The Quest for

Serenity in World Religions

Other books from the same Author

- **Dharma, The Categorial Imperative**; edited by Ashok Vohara, Arvind Sharma and Mrinal Miri; ISBN 81-246-0270-0
- **A New Curve in the Ganges** — Mahatma Gandhi's Interpretation of Hinduism; by Arvind Sharma; ISBN 81-246-0271-9
- **New Focus on Hindu Studies**; by Arvind Sharma; ISBN 81-246-0307-3
- **Sea-shell as Silver** — A Metaphorical Excursion into Advaita Vedānta; by Arvind Sharma; ISBN 81-246-0352-9
- **The World as Dream**; by Arvind Sharma; ISBN 81-246-0365-0
- **The World as Image**; by Arvind Sharma; ISBN 81-246-0362-6

The Quest for Serenity in World Religions

Arvind Sharma
McGill University

D.K. Printworld (P) Ltd.
New Delhi

Cataloging in Publication Data — DK
[Courtesy: D.K. Agencies (P) Ltd. <docinfo@dkagencies.com>]

Sharma, Arvind, 1940-
The quest for serenity in world religions / Arvind Sharma.
viii, 80 p., 22 cm.
Includes bibliograpical references (p.)
Includes index.
ISBN 8124604207

1. Religions. 2. Peace — Religious aspects. I. Title.

DDC 200 22

ISBN 81-246-0420-7
First published in India in 2007

Published and printed by:
D.K. Printworld (P) Ltd.
Regd. Office: 'Sri Kunj', F-52, Bali Nagar
Ramesh Nagar Metro Station
New Delhi-110 015
Phones: (011) 2545-3975; 2546-6019; *Fax*: (011) 2546-5926
E-mail: dkprintworld@vsnl.net
Website: www.dkprintworld.com

Preface

WHAT is your favourite emotion?

The answer would perhaps depend on the person asked, and on the situation in life the person happens to be negotiating at that time, but it is likely that whatever the choice, it will probably be a positive emotion. That is to say, it is likely to be love rather than hatred, hope rather than despair, patience rather than anger, restraint rather than indulgence and so on.

The world religions are united in appealing to such positive emotions. Some scholars have even argued that both the Eastern and the Western religious traditions often opt for essentially the same positive emotions, although the manner in which they do this may have prevented the point from becoming obvious and has to be argued for. Huston Smith makes this point in his response to the following question by Jeffrey Kane: Would you say there are certain universals one would find through many of the world's religions?[1] His response runs as follows:

> Yes. Two levels need to be distinguished here. The one which is the more explicit is what we should do, but beyond that is the question of the kind of person we should try to become.

1. Phil Cousineau, ed., *The Way Things Are: Conversations with Huston Smith on the Spiritual Life*, Berkeley: University of California Press, 2003, p. 205.

> Now, on the first level, what we should do, there are four problem areas in human life that have to be dealt with. These are: violence, wealth, the spoken word and sex. In lower forms of life these problem areas are monitored quite adequately by instinct. Man, though, is an animal without instincts, so these problem areas can get out of hand. Moral precepts are devised to secure appropriate, life-sustaining behaviour in the four areas, and they are remarkably uniform across cultures: don't murder, don't steal, don't lie, don't commit adultery. These are the basic guidelines concerning human behaviour.[2]

He then goes on to say:

> As for the kind of person we should try to become, the virtues point the way. In the West these are commonly identified as humility, charity, and veracity. Humility has nothing to do with low self-esteem; it is to recognize oneself as one and fully one but not more than one, just as charity is to look upon your neighbour as fully one (with all the rights and privileges pertaining thereto) just as you are one. Veracity begins with not being deceitful, but it ends in the sublime objectivity that sees things exactly as they are, undistorted by our subjective preferences. These are the virtues in the West. Asia, interestingly, has the same three but enters them by the back door, so to speak, by speaking of the three poisons — traits that keep the virtues from flourishing in us. The three are: greed (the opposite of humility), hatred (the opposite of charity), and delusion (the opposite of veracity). To the extent that we expunge these three poisons, the virtues will flood our lives automatically. The convergence of East and West in these areas is remarkable.[3]

---

2. Ibid., p. 205.
3. Ibid., p. 205-06.

It's a pity that serenity does not find a place in this list along with humility, charity and veracity. I hope this book helps to demonstrate that the quest for serenity is as much a part of world religions as the search for the other virtues. Alternatively, one could argue that if world religions are engaged in the quest for reality at the metaphysical level, and in the quest for virtue at the moral level, then they are equally engaged in the quest for serenity at the psychological level.

Religion plays many roles but surely one key role which it plays in our lives is to try to beckon us to the shore of serenity, when we find ourselves being tossed to and fro on the stormy sea of life. Every world religion offers a similar hope and yet in its own unique way; each throws out a life-line to us but these lines have their own texture.

This book is an attempt to chart this quest of serenity in world religions, wherein a common pattern seems to underlie this quest for serenity. It seems as if whatever goes on in life can be placed into two distinct dynamic categories: (1) that which we can control, and (2) that which we cannot control. And that life achieves a serene balance if we actively pursue those aspects of life which lie under our will, and graciously accept as the will of God, or of some higher force or power, over which we have no control.

Contents

1

The Quest for Serenity in Hinduism

SERENITY is a much valued virtue in the Hindu religious tradition; as a matter of fact it is required as much of God as of his devotees. Two instances from Hindu mythology should serve to establish this point. The first one relates to the conduct of a sage who once became enraged with the god Viṣṇu and kicked him on the chest. At this god Viṣṇu grabbed hold of his feet and solicitously inquired "I hope your foot is not hurt."[1] This incident is such a celebrated one in Hindu mythology that the standard iconic representation of god Viṣṇu actually depicts the mark resulting from this pedal assault on the God by the sage.[2] The other example is provided by the same god Viṣṇu in his human incarnation as the hero Rāma. Viṣṇu, in his incarnation as Rāma, was born as a prince and when he came of age he was to be crowned the heir-apparent. This would normally be seen as a cause for rejoicing on anyone's part. Before the events could reach such a happy consummation, however, fate intervened. The king was polygamous; he had three wives, and although Rāma was the eldest and very popular, one of the wives wanted her son to inherit the throne. She had in fact saved the king's life twice

1. Benjamin Walker, *The Hindu World*, vol. 2, New York: Frederick A. Praeger, 1968, p. 151.
2. This has been overlooked by some scholars; ibid., vol. II, p. 576.

in the past and on each occasion the king had granted her a boon on which she had taken a rain check. She decided to cash in on them now and demanded (1) that Rāma be banished for fourteen years and (2) that her son be crowned as the heir-apparent. The younger brother declined to be crowned the heir-apparent in the highly idealistic setting of the epic *Rāmāyaṇa*, in which these events are narrated, and Rāma, despite vigorous dissuasion, went into voluntary exile to honour his father's word to his step-mother. The famous redaction of this Sanskrit epic in Hindi was carried out by Tulasīdās (*c.* 1532-1623). The poet remarked that this sudden fluctuation of fortune left Rāma unmoved and goes on to pray for the God's benediction in these words:

> May the brightness of the lotus face of Raghunandana (Rāma), that knew no joy at his enthronement, no melancholy at his sad exile to the forest, ever bring me perfect bliss.[3]

Such serenity may come easily to God, but what of us ordinary mortals?

Hinduism maps out several roads to the achievement of such serenity and while it will not be possible to cover all the approaches within the short compass of this chapter it may be useful to highlight those which are most often drawn upon by Hindus to gain such serenity.

One Hindu doctrine which is helpful in achieving serenity is that of *karma*. There are several formulations of this doctrine, but a common core is represented by the idea that anything that happens to us is ultimately the consequence of our own doing in this life or another previous to this. This applies to both good and evil deeds. Since typically we lose serenity in

---

3. W. Douglas O. Hill, *The Holy Lake of the Acts of Rama*, Delhi: Oxford University Press, 1971, p. 162.

the face of adversity, this doctrine often helps one adjust to it by explaining it as a result of one's own deeds and not the result of mere chance.

> It is this conviction that there are in reality no iniquities in life which explains the absence of any feeling of bitterness — so apt to follow in the wake of pain and sorrow — which is noticeable in India when any misfortune befalls the people. They blame neither God nor their neighbour, but only themselves for it. In fact, this frame of mind, which belief in the *karma* doctrine produces, is one of the most wholesome among its consequences. Deussen refers thus to the case of a blind person whom we met during his India tour: "Not knowing that he had been blind from birth, I sympathized with him and asked by what unfortunate accident the loss of sight had come upon him. Immediately and without showing any sign of bitterness, the answer was ready to his lips, 'By some crime committed in a former birth.'"[4]

It could, of course, be argued that such an attitude encourages pessimism. It, however, certainly encourages resignation and serenity in the face of adversity. Strange though it sounds, it seems reassuring to know that our calamities have not been heaped on us by blind chance or the whim of a capricious god, but are ultimately traceable to ourselves. It also keeps us from blaming others for our failures and encourages better instead of bitter interpersonal relations. It is an interesting reflection, though, that a complete acceptance of predeterminism in any form — whether such predetermination is traced to us or someone else — has the effect of inducing serenity, if at the cost of energy.

---

4. M. Hiriyanna, *The Essentials of Indian Philosophy*, London: George Allen & Unwin Ltd., 1949, pp. 48-49.

An idea concomitant with that of *karma*, namely that of rebirth, also serves to generate serenity. Failure and frustration tend to affect serenity adversely but these tensions usually arise in the context of a limited time span. If, however, one believes in reincarnation then scope for several soothing approaches is thereby created. For one, failure is never final. One always has another chance. For another, one need not feel unduly pressed upon by the limitations of a lifetime as one can see one's effort as extending over several lifetimes. The problem symbolized by the Leaning Tower of Pisa — what if one has the inclination but not the time — is thereby solved.

The doctrine of *karma* and rebirth is common to Hinduism and Buddhism. In fact, it is shared by two other religions of Indian origin — Jainism and Sikhism — as well. It therefore seems to represent a milestone in the search for serenity in India a long time ago, perhaps as early as the eighth century BCE, and with all its drawbacks, seems to have served its people right down to the present day. A hippie of the 1960s, who gets over his breakdown of the car on the highway by attributing it to his "bad *karma*," has distinguished philosophical precedents of which he may only be dimly aware.

The doctrine of *karma* and rebirth is then a remarkable feature of what has been called the Indic religious tradition and to that extent provides a peculiarly Indian approach to the achievement of serenity. This should not lead one to imagine, however, that it is the only approach that has been tried in Hinduism. An approach which Hinduism shares with many other religions (but not with Buddhism and Jainism), is the one associated with theism.

The theistic, or more specifically, the monotheistic world-view is one of those which appeared in the history of mankind at a fairly early stage, probably some time in the second millennium BCE and has proved fruitful and persistent. According to this view, a supreme deity, omniscient, omnipotent, omnipresent, is watching out for us as a father or a mother watches out for the children. So long as one has faith in such a God, one feels serene in the loving protection of such a God. What then is the problem? The problem is that God sometimes tests our faith by allowing adversity to overtake us. Some might even say that we test the faith of God in us by the kinds of things we do. The secret then is to maintain a serene confidence in God's providence. The basic human situation could be theistically interpreted as follows: imperfect man does what he can but because he is imperfect he keeps getting into trouble and God in his perfection and in his kindness saves him from the trouble he keeps getting into.

The faith in such a caring God is bound to generate serenity; the greater the faith, the greater the serenity. There are accounts which illustrate both the depth of faith and the depth of serenity such an outlook promotes. Here is one of them:

Footprints

> One night a man had a dream. He dreamed he was walking along the beach with the LORD. Across the sky flashed scenes from his life. For each scene, he noticed two sets of footprints in the sand; one belonged to him, and the other to the LORD.
>
> When the last scene of his life flashed before him, he looked back at the footprints in the sand. He noticed that many times along the path of his life there was only one set of footprints. He also noticed that it happened at the very lowest and saddest times in his life.

This really bothered him and he questioned the LORD about it: "LORD, you said that once I decided to follow you, you'd walk with me all the way. But I have noticed that during the most troublesome times in my life, there is only one set of footprints. I don't understand why when I needed you most you would leave me."

The LORD replied, "My precious child, I love you and would never leave you. During your times of trial and suffering, when you see only one set of footprints, it was then that I carried you."[5]

---

5. Source Unknown. This form of theistic Hinduism sometimes takes the form of attributing all that one experiences in this life to the will of God. Needless to say, this attitude brings with it a serenity of its own.

All His Will

There is a man who was intensely devoted to Śrī Rāma and he believed that nothing could happen in the world without His Will and that His Will was the ultimate cause for every action of his and every step that he took. Once he was passing through a forest when he found some decoits returning with the booty after committing a dacoity. Seeing him they told him to carry their booty and placed a heavy load upon his head. He went with them but a party of policemen came and when the decoits saw them coming, they ran away in different directions leaving him behind with the booty on is head. The police arrested him and brought him to the police station and after a trial he was sent to a jail. When he was released after his term of imprisonment he came home to his village. The people of the village asked why he had been absent for such a long period. He said, "Everything has happened by Rāma's Will. By Rāma's Will I passed by a lonely road in a forest and by Rāma's Will I was seized by a band of decoits and asked to carry their booty. By Rāma's Will the police came and the decoits ran away, leaving me behind. By Rāma's Will I was arrested, tried, and sentenced and by Rāma's Will, having served my term, I have been released and have come home. — Swami Sambuddhananda, *Vedanta Through Stories*, Bombay: Sri Ramakrishna Ashram, 1959, pp. 192-93.

The Hindu text, the *Bhagavad-Gītā*, provides a good illustration of the overcoming of anxiety through devotion to God. In that popular text a warrior is called upon to engage in a battle which will involve the slaughter of his own kinsmen and this fills him with anxiety. God who happens to be acting as his charioteer on this occasion tries to relieve his anxiety by several arguments but when all else fails discloses this secret of serenity — surrender to God (XVIII: 64-66):

> Further, the highest secret of all,
> My supreme message, hear.
> Because thou are greatly loved of Me,
> Therefore I shall tell thee what is good for thee.
>
> Be Me-minded, devoted to me;
> Worshipping Me, revere Me;
> And to Me alone shalt thou go; truly to thee
> I promise it — (because) thou art dear to Me.
>
> Abandoning all (other) duties,
> Go to Me as thy sole refuge;
> From all evils I thee
> Shall rescue: be not grieved![6]

Later tradition was to dispute whether man needs to make any effort to surrender or whether God's grace envelops him completely. The two positions came to be known, somewhat quaintly, as monkey-logic and cat-logic. The young of the monkey has to cling to the mother as she moves from branch to branch and tree to tree. Thus although there is dependence on the mother, some co-operation on the part of the young is involved in the course of arboreal locomotion. The way the cat handles its young is very different. The mother lifts the

---

6. Franklin Edgerton, tr., *The Bhagavad-Gītā*, Part I, Cambridge, Massachusetts: Harvard University Press, 1946, p. 177.

young with her mouth and moves them around without the kitten having to do anything whatsoever. The dependence on the mother is complete. However one may choose to rely on God, it is clear that this is one way of achieving serenity.

A third approach to developing serenity also appeared in Hinduism very early and later on came to be identified as non-dualism or monism. Just as monotheism represents the belief that there is only one God, monism represents the belief that there is only one reality. But whereas belief in one God involves the idea of a created universe and its creatures existing outside of that God, the idea of one reality allows for no such exclusion of anything outside that reality. This, of course, at once raises the question: but we see multiplicity of people and objects around us all the time, so how can there be just one unitary reality. Monistic Hinduism makes precisely this apparently absurd claim, comparable to the "scandal of the Cross" in its engaging outrageousness, and much of monistic thought in Hinduism is devoted to tackling precisely this problem. One of the standard answers has been that the plurality is not real but only an appearance, of the nature of a superimposition on the single reality, just as one might superimpose the vision of a snake on a rope and become anxiety-ridden on account of one's ignorance of the true nature of the rope.

But how does monism lead to a serene life? The cue is provided by a brief but significant statement in an early Hindu religious text which says: "It is from the presence of the other that fear rises."[7] If, however, according to monism, there is no other, for there is only one reality, the ontological basis of anxiety is thereby destroyed and a case for unfailing serenity established (provided of course that the premise is true). One

---

7. *Bṛhadāraṇyaka Upaniṣad*, I.4.2.

may however discover that such a basis for serenity is so profound as to threaten our serenity itself and when the idea is first explained by a sage for the benefit of his wife (whom he is about to leave) she admits to being bewildered like us. But the sage explains serenely:

> For where there is a duality, as it were, there one sees another; there one smells another; there one tastes another; there one speaks to another; there one hears another; there one thinks of another; there one touches another; there one understands another. But where everything has become just one's own self, then whereby and whom would one see? then whereby and whom would one smell? then whereby and whom would one taste? then whereby and whom would one speak? then whereby and whom would one hear? then whereby and whom would one think? then whereby and whom would one touch? then whereby and whom would one understand? Whereby would one understand him by means of whom one understands this All?[8]

The question arises: if there is only one undifferentiated reality, then what is the ontological status of the events we seem to experience in the world of multiplicity. The problem is a matter of much philosophical debate, but one point is clear: their status has to be less than that of something "ultimately" real, no matter how real they appear to us. It is often said that they are of the nature of dream — indeed.

The World is but a Dream

> A son was born to a king. He was the only child and was therefore "the apple of the eye" of both the king and the queen. The prince became a favourite with all and as he

---

8. Robert Ernest Hume, tr., *The Thirteen Principal Upaniṣads*, London: Oxford University Press, 1968, p. 147.

> grew older he was taught all the arts and the sciences. One day, all of a sudden, the prince fell ill. The malady went on getting worse and even the best physician of the kingdom found that all treatments were of no avail. Both the king and the queen never left his side day and night and the most competent physician and nurses continuously attended to him. The king was exhausted by his constant vigil and one night he could not resist falling asleep. He was awakened by the sound of crying and weeping and learnt that the prince had passed away while he was asleep. The king sat as if he was stupefied, without speaking a single word. The queen asked him how it was that on the passing of the only child whom he loved so much there was not a single drop of tear in his eye. The king said, "O queen, when I fell asleep I dreamt that I had become the monarch of a larger kingdom, much larger than mine, and the father of seven worthy and ideal princes, each of whom was well trained in the art of administration. I handed over the charge of my kingdom to them and thereafter I was spending my days in peace and happiness with you. And now this tragedy has taken place and I am unable to make up my mind whether I should lament for the child that has left us today or whether I should mourn the loss of the seven sons and a vast kingdom. I see no difference in the two bereavements and to me the world has become nothing but a dream."[9]

We have now discussed three ways in which Hindus have sought serenity — through detached action, through simple faith and through philosophical insight. These approaches within the tradition are respectively described as those of *karma* (here meaning action rather than the Law of *karma*), *Bhakti* (devotion) and *jñāna* (intuitive knowledge). Sometimes the word *yoga* is added to these terms so that they are called

9. Swami Sambuddhananda, op. cit., pp. 44-45.

karmayoga, *bhaktiyoga* and *jñānayoga*. Why this emphasis on *yoga*? Could it be that it might also offer an approach to serenity by itself?

Yoga helps us to realize the reality of the universe and put us at ease inasmuch as our lack of serenity reflects a cosmic uneasiness with our situation. But the same word is also used for techniques which ease our mind in a less cosmic dimension. These practices are based on the recognition of the close connection between physical and mental states and the ability of one to induce the other. Thus sitting quietly for a while tends to compose the mind just as the removal of mental tension puts the body at ease. This insight is of considerable help in maintaining serenity in the rough-and-tumble of daily living. When mental factors tend to disrupt serenity, disciplining the body helps maintain balance. Similarly, when physical factors disrupt serenity, the cultivation of the right mental attitude reduces the amplitude of disturbance.

In Hinduism, therefore, serenity is sought and obtained through *yoga* in one form or another.

Some lofty philosophy and arduous pursuit of *yoga* are not the only resources for cultivating serenity available within Hinduism. A more popular avenue to it is provided by such stories that propound the view that everything happens for the best.

2

The Quest for Serenity in Buddhism

THE quest for serenity in Buddhism is rooted in its very origin. According to the traditional accounts, Buddha was leading the pleasant life of a prince of his times when the harsher realities of existence intruded into his life, destroying his serenity, at least temporarily. The encounter of the prince with a sick man, an old man and a dead man is said to have roused him from his princely complacency into abandoning the royal lifestyle and donning the robes of a monk. After the Buddha has attained realization he embarked on a missionary career. The descriptions of the Buddha in the Buddhist texts emphasize his cheerfulness of countenance and the serenity of his demeanor. How then is this serenity to be attained through Buddhism?

At one level the steps suggested are fairly simple though this does not necessarily make them easy. They consist of eliminating negative thoughts from the mind and supplanting them by positive ones. Thus Buddhism emphasizes the four sublime meditations. Firstly, one fills one's mind and heart with thoughts of *friendliness towards all living beings.* One radiates good will. Then one similarly suffuses oneself with a *compassion for all living beings.* As a further step one rejoices in the *happiness of others.* A little reflection will subject that one of the sentiments corrosive of serenity is jealousy — feeling lousy over someone else's happiness. In the Buddhist meditation the process is reversed and one is deliberately encouraged to participate vicariously in the happiness of others. Finally one cultivates *equanimity as a mental attitude*. This might appear initially puzzling. For instance, it is easy to see how friendliness, compassion and participatory joy can lead to serenity in our dealings with living beings who constitute our environment. But is not equanimity too much like indifference? Anyone can gain serenity at the price of cruel indifference. Such a viewpoint however misses the Buddhist perspective on the issue. For one thing, the equanimity being talked about here does not consist in indifference to the sufferings of others but to our own. It is the ability of the mind to rise above the petty fluctuations of mood that sometimes plague daily living. Moreover, consider the doctor or the surgeon. In a professional situation it is the patient who is usually distraught and it is the doctor who is composed, who is equanimous. Does it mean that he is indifferent to the suffering of the patient? On the contrary. It is precisely because he is equanimous that he can remove that suffering.

It is clear then that one way whereby serenity can be gained in Buddhism is by the cultivation of benign mental attitudes. In this it conforms to common sense, as also in hinting that a cool rationality is also conducive to serenity. This point is made in a story regarding a previous existence of the Buddha and is used by Erich Fromm to excellent effect.

> Once a hare sat under a mango tree and slept. Suddenly he heard a loud noise. He thought the world was coming to an end and started to run. When the other hares saw him running they asked, "Why do you run so fast?" He replied, "The world is coming to an end." Upon which the deer joined them in their flight. Thus one species after another joined the animals already running until the whole animal kingdom was in panicky flight which would have ended in

> its destruction. When Buddha, who at the time was living as a wise man in one of his many forms of existence, saw all the animals running in their panic he asked the last group that had joined the flight why they were running. "Because the world is coming to an end," they answered. "This cannot be true," Buddha said. "The world is not coming to an end. Let us find out why they think so." He then inquired of one species after another, tracing the rumour back to the deer and then at last to the hares. When the hares told him that they were running because the world was coming to an end, he asked which particular hare had told them so. They pointed to the one who had started the report, and Buddha turned to him and asked, "Where were you and what did you do when you thought the world was coming to an end?" The hare answered, "I was sitting under a mango tree and was asleep." "You probably heard a mango fruit fall," Buddha told him. "The noise awakened you, you got frightened and thought the world was coming to an end. Let us go back to the tree where you sat and find out whether this was so." They both went to the tree. They found that indeed a mango had fallen where the hare had sat. Thus Buddha saved the animal kingdom from destruction.[1]

The two methods considered so far for gaining serenity according to Buddhism are fairly straightforward and in accord with common sense and daily experience. But the central method which Buddhism recommends for attaining serenity is highly radical and almost revolutionary to the point of at least initially inducing anxiety rather than serenity. It is predicated on the Buddhist doctrine that our concept of "I" is a case of false understanding — that there is no person apart from our feelings, thoughts, etc. which we mistakenly attribute

---

1. Erich Fromm, *Psychoanalysis and Religion,* New Haven: Yale University Press, 1950, pp. 39-40.

to this person. And if there is no self, who is there in reality to feel anxiety and even really need serenity? No one.

This is how Buddhist doctrine cuts the Gordian knot philosophically. But let us go back and unravel the Buddhist position psychologically. One must here begin by recognizing how vital the psychological implications are. This is well-illustrated by another story from the Buddha's previous existence. This time he is said to have been a sage living in a hermitage when a king entered it with his wives on a hunting expedition. In the course of events the king formed the suspicion that the sage had been flirting with his wives and had him hacked to pieces. This is the crucial moment in the narrative. While narrating it the Buddha points out that at the moment he was being dismembered he had to keep himself disabused of the idea of a self, a being, a soul or a person. "If I had had such notions then I would also have felt ill-will at that time."[2]

This might appear a bit far-fetched and exaggerated but the Buddhist idea of a lack of self is so contrary to our ingrained notions that such excesses are probably required to shake us to a contrary conception. In any case the implication of such a view of the human personality for the cultivation of serenity can be spelled out in some detail now. Basically our anxiety results from failure to dichotomize emotions. Let us suppose that I get angry. On a superficial level a single event has occurred — I have become enraged. On a more careful view, according to Buddhism, two events have been conflated: (1) the emotion of anger has made its appearance and (2) "I" have appropriated that emotion of anger as my own so that instead of there just being anger floating around, so to say, I

2. Edward Conze, "Buddhism: The Mahayana" in R.C. Zaehner, ed., *The Concise Encyclopaedia of Living Faiths*, Boston: Beacon Press, 1967, p. 304.

have become angry. Buddhist meditation attaches great significance to distinguishing our sense of self from our perceptions, feelings, thoughts, etc. According to early Buddhist philosophy these perceptions, feelings, etc. do exist in their own realms but loss of serenity results from our appropriation of them. A common experience lends some credence to this view. The moment a person realizes that he or she is angry, or says so, the person becomes more serene and is less likely to throw the T.V. out of the window than before. Buddhist philosophy makes the further point that when we say "I" am angry, this "I" is a misnomer, so that there is in reality, apart from our mistaken notion of self, no one to get angry!

There are thus two procedures involved here: (1) dissociating the emotion from the "self" and (2) realizing the true nature of the self. The second step is abstruse but it is easier to relate to the first one, though often the two are discussed together, as for instance in a famous discourse of the Buddha on mindfulness. On the questions of feelings for instance, the Buddha advises the *bhikkhus* or monks to observe feelings as feelings, not as *his* feelings.

> And how *Bhikhus*, does a *bhikhu* live observing feelings?
>
> Here, *bhikhus*, a *bhikhu* when experiencing a pleasant feeling knows: "I experience a pleasant feeling"; when experiencing a painful feeling, he knows: "I experience a painful feeling: when experiencing a neither-pleasant-nor-painful feeling, he knows: I experience a neither-pleasant-nor-painful feeling." When experiencing a pleasant worldly feeling, he knows: "I experience a pleasant worldly feeling"; when experiencing a pleasant spiritual feeling, he knows: "I experience a pleasant spiritual feeling"; when experiencing a painful worldly feeling he knows: "I experience a painful worldly feeling"; when experiencing a painful spiritual

> feeling he knows: "I experience a painful spiritual feeling"; when experiencing a neither-pleasant-nor-painful worldly feeling he knows: "I experience a neither-pleasant-nor-painful worldly feeling"; when he experiences a neither-pleasant-nor-painful spiritual feeling he knows: "I experience a neither-pleasant-nor-painful spiritual feeling."
>
> He lives in this way observing feelings internally, or externally, or . . . internally and externally. He lives observing origination-factors in feelings, or dissolution-factors in feelings, or origination-and-dissolution-factors in feelings. Or his mindfulness is established to the extent necessary just for knowledge and awareness that feeling exists, and he lives unattached, and clings to naught in the world. In this way, *bhikkhus*, a *bhikkhu* lives observing feelings.[3]

Thus far we have identified four steps towards the achievement of serenity recommended in Buddhism: (1) the sublime meditations; (2) rationality; (3) the disappropriation of emotions and (4) the realization of the artificial nature of the ego. Before one adds another element to the list, the last point may be clarified further. Many have had trouble throughout history philosophically with the Buddhist view that man has no real "self," "ego," or "person." But psychologically the point is less hard to grasp if it is observed that we are usually most serene when least obsessed with our ego or self. The more we de-individuate ourselves the more serene we are likely to be.

At a less abstruse level the Buddhists identify the mind as the source of anxiety and its proper cultivation the path to serenity. Here again however we may distinguish between philosophy and psychology. Some Buddhist thinkers identify the mind as the primal principle. Thus the story is told of the

3. Walpola Rahula, *What the Buddha Taught*, New York: Grove Press Inc., 1974, p. 113.

Chinese sage who in his search for truth ended up sharing camp with robbers and thieves and one night shocked them all by leaping from his cot with the affirmation: "It is the mind." Hard as it is to remain serene in the face of so startling a declaration we shall endeavour to do so and pass on to the enigmatic episode associated with Bodhidharma, the founder of Zen Buddhism in China according to tradition. The incident has a direct bearing on the issue of serenity, showing that anxiety can be much ado about nothing.

> Bodhidharma sits facing the wall. His future successor stands in the snow and presents his severed arm to Bodhidharma. He cries: "My mind is not pacified. Master, pacify my mind."
>
> Bodhidharma says: "If you bring me that mind, I will pacify it for you."
>
> The successor says: "When I search my mind I cannot hold it."
>
> Bodhidharma says: "Then your mind is pacified already."[4]

---

4. Paul Reps, compiler, *Zen Flesh, Zen Bones*, New York: Doubleday and Company Inc./Anchor Books, 1961, pp. 121-22. Should one wish to pursue the point further the following account is instructive (ibid., pp. 38-39):

> Joshua began the study of Zen when he was sixty years old and continued until he was eighty, when he realized Zen.
>
> He taught from the age of eighty until he was one hundred and twenty.
>
> A student once asked him: "If I haven't anything in my mind, what shall I do?"
>
> Joshua replied: "Throw it out."
>
> "But if I haven't anything, how can I throw it out?" continued the questioner.
>
> " 'Well,' said Joshua, 'then carry it out.' "

It is clear then that Buddhism recommends two distinguishable but not necessarily different routes to the attainment of serenity — one which focuses on the mind and generates serenity by cultivating its sublimity, rationality or purity, and the other which dissects personality like an onion till the core turns out to be no-core and the very agent is shown to be really absent. Such anxiety in absentia being a logical impossibility, serenity follows. This point is well illustrated by the following Zen anecdote: "Yamaoka Tesshu, as a young student of Zen, visited one master after another. He called upon Dokuon of Shokoku.

> Desiring to show his attainment, he said: "The mind, Buddha, and sentient beings, after all, do not exist. The true nature of phenomena is emptiness. There is no realization, no delusion, no sage, no mediocrity. There is no giving and nothing to be received."
>
> Dokuon, who was smoking quietly, said nothing. Suddenly he whacked Yamaoka with his bamboo pipe. This made the youth quite angry.
>
> "If nothing exists," inquired Dukuon, "where did this anger come from?"[5]

---

5. Ibid., pp. 69-70.

3

The Quest for Serenity in Confucianism

CONFUCIANISM is often regarded as more of an ethic than a religion but in either case the search for the serene life cannot be dissociated from it. As a matter of fact, its founder, Confucius or Kung-Fu-Tze, is considered more or less a failure in his own lifetime. He may even have regarded himself as such, for it is said that he died a disappointed man.

> The great mountain must crumble, the strong beam must break, and the wise man wither away like a plant.[1]

The phenomenal success we associate with him — that of virtually laying down the pattern for a normative life for almost a quarter of the world for two thousand years — was posthumous. It would not be without interest, therefore, to see how he faced failure and distress in his own life. At one level it is perhaps thus expressed in one of his sayings: "I will not grieve that men do not know me; I will grieve that I do not know men."[2] But Confucius also invoked a higher principle in this context — that of T'ien or Heaven.

---

1. Cited in Will Durant, *Our Oriental Heritage,* New York: Simon and Schuster, 1954, p. 664.
2. Cited in Huston Smith, *The Religions of Man,* New York: Harper & Row, Perennial Library Edition, 1965, p. 165.

In Confucius' own life the search for serenity is closely associated with the will of Heaven. The following passages from the *Analects* could be cited in this respect:

> The Master said, Heaven begat the power (*te*) that is in me. What have I to fear from such a one as Huan T'ui? — VII:22
>
> When the Master was trapped in Ku'ang, he said, when King Wen perished, did that mean that culture (*wen*) ceased to exist? If Heaven had really intended that such culture as his should disappear, a later-day mortal would never have been able to link himself to it as I have done. And if Heaven does not intend to destroy such culture, what have I to fear from the people of K'uang? — IX.5
>
> When Yen Hui died, the Master said, Alas, Heaven has bereft me, Heaven has bereft me! — IX.8
>
> The Master said, the truth is, no one knows me! Tzu-kung said, What is the reason that you are not known? The Master said, I do not "accuse Heaven, nor do I lay the blame on men." But the studies of men here below are felt on high, and perhaps after all I am known; not here, but in Heaven! — XIV.37
>
> Kung-po Liao spoke against Tzu-lu to the Chi Family. Tzu-lu Ching-po informed the Master saying, I fear my master's mind has been greatly unsettled by this. But in the case of Kung-po Liao, I believe my influence is still great enough to have his carcass exposed in the market-place. The Master said, If it is the will of Heaven that the Way shall prevail, then the Way will prevail. But if it is the will of Heaven that the Way should perish, then it must needs perish. What can Kung-po Liao do against Heaven's will? — XIV.38[3]

3. Arthur Waley, tr., *The Analects of Confucius*, New York: Random House, 1938, pp. 127, 139, 154, 189-90.

There is a clear tendency to relate to Heaven as a higher referent, in relation to which the oscillations of fortune can be viewed more steadily. Confucius' own brilliant autobiographical summation of his own spiritual development relates it to Heaven:

> The Master said, at fifteen I set my heart upon learning. At thirty, I had planted my feet firm upon the ground. At forty, I no longer suffered from perplexities. At fifty, I knew what were the biddings of Heaven. At sixty, I heard them with docile ear. At seventy, I could follow the dictates of my own heart; for what I desired no longer overstepped the boundaries of right.[4]

It has been suggested on the basis of this passage that submission to the Will of Heaven was "a hard lesson that Confucius himself did not master till the age of fifty."[5]

This distinction between what one does oneself and what Heaven does to one turned out to be a crucial one in the doctrine regarding serenity in Confucianism. As already seen, its germs are clearly present in the life of Confucius. Broadly speaking, the events of life can be classified into two categories: (1) those over which we have control and (2) those over which we do not have control. Thus it is within our power to be kind to our children, but perhaps not within our power to prevent an earthquake or an untimely death. The example of Confucius' life seems to suggest that serenity could be achieved by acting virtuously in the sphere over which we had control as the "Will of Heaven" which served some higher

---

4. Ibid., p. 88.
5. Ibid., p. 41. But also see A.C. Graham, "Confucianism," in R.C. Zaehner, ed., *The Concise Encyclopaedia of Living Faiths*, Boston: Beacon Press, 1967, p. 381.

movements are complementary. "The world is at war, says Confucius, because its constituent states are improperly governed." These constituent units must be in harmony for serenity to be realized, just as serenity must reign within the constituent units for overall harmony to be realized.

The search for serenity in Confucianism then consisted of accepting (1) the will of Heaven; (2) the will of a just government; (3) the will of the paterfamilias and (4) cultivating those personal virtues which induced serenity. Before one elaborates on the last of these, it may be pointed out that the acceptance of the Will of Heaven, or the Government or the head of the family did not mean blind acceptance of their fiat, but rather an enlightened obedience. Protest was possible. In the case of Heaven one would be hard put to pursue the point further but interesting examples are forthcoming of how submission was not to be confused with serenity in the other cases. It was not considered improper, for instance, to resist injustice: "When the command is wrong, a son should resist his father, and a minister should resist his august Master."[9]

The scope for misunderstanding some of the Confucian techniques for the search for serenity being removed, or at least reduced, one may now turn to the personal attitudes he recommended as conducive to it. Scholars speak of a set of five virtues in this regard. The pentad according to the classical formulation consists of *jen*, "benevolence," which shows itself, according to Mencius (*Mencius*, iia.6), in the feeling of sympathy for others; *yi*, "duty," reflected in the feeling of shame after a wrong action; *li*, "manners," propriety, good form, reflected in the feeling of deference; *chih*, "wisdom," reflected in the sense of right and wrong; and *hsin*, good faith,

9. Ibid., p. 13.

trustworthiness, for which no corresponding feeling is given by Mencius.[10]

Some modern scholars offer the following mix: "*jen, chun-tzu, li* and *wen* — goodness, the gentleman, government by virtue, and the arts of peace — such were the values to which Confucius had given his heart."[11]

But central and crucial to both is the virtue of *jen*.

> *Jen*, etymologically a combination of the character for "man" and for "two," names the ideal relationship which should pertain between people. Variously translated as goodness, man-to-manness, benevolence, and love, it is perhaps best rendered as human-heartedness. *Jen* was the virtue of virtues in Confucius' view of life. It was a sublime even transcendental perfection that he confessed he had never seen fully incarnated. Involving as it does the display of human capacities at their best, it is a virtue so exalted that one "cannot but be chary in speaking of it." To the noble it is dearer than life itself. "The determined scholar and the man of *Jen* . . . will even sacrifice their lives to preserve their *Jen* complete."[12]

How this virtue enabled the disciples of Confucius to achieve serenity can be gauged from the following passage in the *Analects*:

> Ssu-ma Niu grieved, saying, Everyone else has brothers; I alone have none. Tzu-hsia said, I have heard this saying, "Death and life are the decree of Heaven; wealth and rank depend on the will of Heaven. If a gentleman attends to business and does not idle away his time, if he behaves

---

10. Cited in Will Durant, op. cit., p. 671.
11. A.C. Graham, op. cit., p. 370.
12. Huston Smith, op. cit., p. 187.

is a link in a chain. Perhaps a sense of continuity tends to impart to our daily lives a certain serenity! We saw earlier how in Hinduism and Buddhism our life here was looked upon as a link in a chain of lives which extended into the past and the future. Confucianism does not believe in rebirth, but it did develop an analogous idea. One's life here was seen as constituting a generational link in a chain which extended far into the past and into the future. This reverence for ancestors, especially during the moments of the ceremony, may have lifted their awareness to a higher level of biological if not evolutionary awareness and imparted to it a perspective which must have made some daily anxieties of life a rather picayune.

Thus serenity through Confucianism could be achieved (1) by a proper acceptance of the Order of Heaven; (2) by a proper cultivation of social order; (3) by the cultivation of the virtue of *jen* above all, and (4) by the recognition of one's role as a link in a generational chain which extended far and wide into the past and the future.

4

The Quest for Serenity in Taoism

THE search for serenity in Confucianism seemed to be predicated on a certain clarity — the distinction between what was under one's control and what was not, between "self-control" and "other control." A recognition of this fine distinction enabled one to lead both a serene and virtuous life: serene in its acceptance of the will of Heaven and virtuous in the pursuit of the moral will. The model for the serene life in Taoism is somewhat different and is anchored in the concept of the *yin* and the *yang*. Although the *yin-yang* concept is not absent in Confucianism, its implications are developed and elaborated in Taoism in far greater detail. The standard way of representing this concept is through a diagram which usually takes the following form:

Three key elements need to be borne in mind in analysing the diagram: that the forces are rhythmic, that they are complementary and that they interpenetrate.

A recognition of the rhythmic nature of the forces enables us to respond with serenity to the natural alternations life is subject to. Day is followed by night, summer by winter, rain by dryness and so on. Once these fluctuations are seen as built into the very nature of things, their capacity to bother us is greatly diminished.

A recognition of the complementary nature of the dualities of life is similarly helpful. The death of a dear one would cause loss of serenity. If, however, death is recognized as something which *complements* life, then the trauma is thereby reduced. An extreme case of this is provided by the life of Chuang-Tzu. The account goes that when his wife died and people came to console him, they found him making merry. One of them protested.

> "You lived with her, she brought up your children and grew old," said Hui Tzu. "It should be enough simply not to weep at her death. But pounding on a tub and singing — this is going too far, isn't it?"
>
> Chuang-Tzu replied, "You're wrong. When she first died, do you think I didn't grieve like anyone else? But I looked back to her beginning and the time before she was born. Not only the time before she was born, but the time before she had a body. Not only the time before she had a body, but the time before she had a spirit.
>
> "In the midst of the jumble of wonder and mystery a change took place and she had a spirit. Another change and she had a body. Another change and she was born. Now there's been another change and she's dead. It's just like the progression of the four seasons, spring, summer, fall, winter.

> "Now she's going to lie down peacefully in a vast room. If I were to follow after her bawling and sobbing, it would show that I don't understand anything about fate. So I stopped."
>
> Chapter 2[1]

Another key point to bear in mind is the interpretation of the two elements — the *yin* and the *yang*, unlike the Confucian pattern of the sharp distinction, say between Heaven's will and our own. This interpretation is diagrammatically represented by the presence of the dark spot on the white side and the white spot on the dark side. Thus the day represents the *yang* or male element — but is not purely male for it contains "shadows" which are dark. Similarly, the night represents the *yin* or female element — but it is not purely female for it contains moonlight. Once this interpenetration is recognized, the question naturally arises: how does it contribute to the achievement of serenity?

We are inclined to look upon the happenings in life in terms of good or bad. Something bad happens and we call it a "tough break." Something good happens and we call it a "good break." Yet in point of fact the connections may be far deeper and subtler. The good and bad aspects of life interpenetrate in a way not obvious on the surface. The point is illustrated in Taoism by the anecdote of the farmer whose horse ran away.

> Once upon a time there was a peasant who saved up his money for many years until eventually he had enough to buy a horse. When he returned home from the market leading his new horse his next-door neighbour came in to congratulate him. But the peasant, being a good Taoist, replied, "Who knows what's good and what's bad!"

---

1. T. Patrick Burke, *The Major Religions: An Introduction with Texts*, Oxford: Blackwell Publishers Inc., 1996, p. 139.

> During the night his new horse escaped, and all his savings were lost. His next-door neighbour came in to commiserate with him. But the peasant, being a good Taoist, replied, "Who knows what's good and what's bad!"
>
> The following day the horse returned, bringing with him a wild horse. Quickly the peasant sent his sons out to catch both of them. Now he had two horses. His next-door neighbour came in to congratulate him. But the peasant replied, "Who knows what's good and what's bad!"
>
> The next day his eldest son was outbreaking in the wild horse, when he fell off and broke his leg. The next-door neighbour came in to commiserate with him. But the peasant replied, "Who knows what's good and what's bad!"
>
> Shortly after that the Emperor's army came around seeking conscripts for the war then taking place, and they would have taken the peasant's eldest son, but since he now had a broken leg, he could go free. The next-door neighbour came in to congratulate him. But the peasant replied, "Who knows what's good and what's bad!"
>
> Thus good fortune changes into bad fortune, and bad fortune into good.
>
> — A version of the story
> told in Huai Nan Tzu, chapter 18[2]

Taoism also develops a mystical dimension to it. This tendency is particularly marked in Chuang-Tzu and has the effect of generating a kind of serenity, which comes from a recognition of the evanescence of circumstance. The fugitive nature of human experience can impart to it a dream-like character and this can lead to serenity in two ways — by making us wonder who we really are and by making us wonder what is really happening to us. For if the status of both is in gentle rather

2. Ibid., p. 132.

than anxious doubt then what *happens* to *us,* whose ontological status is thrown in doubt, could be a matter of amusement rather than anxiety. We may refer here to Chuang-tzu's famous dream:

> Once upon a time, Chuang Chou (i.e. Chuang-Tzu) dreamed that he was a butterfly, a butterfly fluttering about, enjoying itself. It did not know that it was Chuang Chou. Suddenly he awoke with a start and he was Chuang Chou again. But he did not know whether he was Chuang Chou who had dreamed that he was a butterfly, or whether he was a butterfly dreaming that he was Chuang Chou. Between Chuang Chou and the butterfly there must be some distinction. This is what is called the transformation of things.[3]

And so far as the ontological status of the universe is concerned, the following Taoist doubts arise.

> How do I know that the love of life is not a delusion? How do I know that he who is afraid of death is not like a man who left his home as a youth and forgot to return? Lady Li was the daughter of the border warden of Ai. When she was first brought to the state of Chin, she wept until the bosom of her robe was drenched with tears. But when she came to the royal residence, shared with the king his luxurious couch and ate sumptuous food, she regretted that she had wept. How do I know that the dead do not repent of their former craving for life? Those who dream of a merry drinking party may the next morning wail and weep. Those who dream of wailing and weeping may in the morning go off gaily to hunt. While they dream they do not know what they are dreaming. In their dream, they may even try to interpret their dream. Only when they have awakened do they begin

3. Wm. Theodore de Bary, et al., op. cit., p. 73.

> to know that they have dreamed. By and by comes the great awakening, and then we shall know that it has all been a great dream. Yet all the while the fools think that they are awake; this they are sure of. With minute nicety, they discriminate between princes and grooms. How stupid! Confucius and you are both in a dream. And when I say that you are in a dream, this is also a dream. This way of talking may be called paradoxical. If after ten thousand generations we could once meet a great sage who knew how to explain the paradox, it would be as though we met him after only one morning or one evening.[4]

Thus both Taoist cosmology and Taoist mysticism may assist one in the search for serenity. A third aspect of Taoism which is equally promising is its strong identification with nature. This is apparent right from the use of natural images like those of water in the Tao Te Ching,[5] the fundamental scripture of Taoism, to Taoist landscape painting.[6] If life and death, which are only the extreme expressions of the vicissitudes of life, are a part of nature of which we are also a part, then such unity can only serve to alleviate anxiety. That even Confucius may not have frowned upon such a search for serenity in communion with nature is evident from the following passage:

> Once when Tzu Lu, Tseng Hsi, Jan Yu, and Kung-hsi Hua were seated in attendance upon him, Confucius said: "You no doubt consider me a day or so your senior, but let us not mind that. When out of office you say among yourselves that your merits are not recognized. Now suppose some prince were to recognize your merits, what would be your wishes?" Tzu Lu without hesitation replied: "Take a

---

4. Ibid., p. 72.
5. See Huston Smith, op. cit., pp. 206-07.
6. Ibid.

> kingdom of a thousand chariots, hemmed in by great powers, oppressed by invading troops, and suffering from famine in addition — I should like to take charge of it. In three years' time I could make it brave and make it understand the right course to pursue." Confucius smiled at him. "And how about you, Ch'iu [Jan Yu]?" "Take a district of sixty or seventy *li* square," answered Jan Yu, "or say, one of fifty or sixty *li* square. I should like to take charge of it. In three years' time I could make its people live in abundance; but as for the promotion of rites (*li*) and music, I should have to leave that to a real gentlemen." "And how about you, Ch'ih (Kung-hsi Hua)?" "Not that I say I could do it," he answered, "but I should like to be trained for it. At the ceremonies in the Ancestral Temple (of the Imperial House) or at the conference of the princes, I should like to wear the ceremonial cap and gown, and be a minor official assisting in the ceremony." "And how about you, Tien (Tseng Hsi)?" Tseng Hsi paused in his playing of the zither. Putting it aside he rose and replied: "I am afraid my wishes are entirely different from those cherished by these three gentlemen." "What harm is there in that?" said Confucius. "We are just trying to let each express his desire." Then he said: "In the later days of spring, when the light spring garments are made, I would like to take along five or six grown-ups and six or seven youths to bathe in the River Yi, and after the bath go to enjoy the breeze in the woods among the altars of Wu-yi, and then a return home, loitering and singing on our way." Confucius heaved a deep sigh and said: "You are the man after my own heart."[7]

There is, however, a difference in the way serenity can be sought. In Hinduism and Buddhism it consists of rising above the vicissitudes of life; in Confucianism it lies in ordering them

---

7. Wm. Theodore de Bary, et al., op. cit., pp. 20-21.

harmoniously, and in Taoism it seems to lie in flowing along with them.

The search for serenity in Taoism continued with its development and assumed several forms. These new forms emerge in the commentaries on the Tao Te Ching and the Chuang-Tzu. Wang Pi, for instance, commented on the Tao Te Ching centuries after Christ and for him the original non-being remained the pivotal concept. For him it meant pure being. This meant that there were no distinctions within it. It was the distinction between Li and Chi or substance and function which was particularly absent. As pure principle it could not go wrong and serenity was achieved in this normative way by being in harmony with it.

As one might well have come to expect by this time, the commentary on the Chuang Tzu by Kuo Hsiang took a different line and emphasized harmony with nature. Thus serenity, which was achieved in Wang Pi by being in accord with the Tao in the transcendent aspect, was achieved in Kuo Hsiang by being in accord with its immanent aspect in nature.

Another approach to serenity took a different route, and represented, along with fatalism, a new development. But before we turn to its consideration the search for serenity by focusing on the third sense of the Tao — the way in which life should be lived to accord with the transcendent and immanent aspects may be examined. The key concept in relation to serenity in Taoism in such a context is the *Wu-Wei,* or no-action, or more properly, not taking any unnatural action. Whereas, in pre-Christian Taoism, such a view of life led to a certain quietism, such was not so in the case of neo-Taoism, which found activism quite consistent with natural action. This seems to reflect a basic division of opinion among many religions as to how serenity may be achieved. In Hinduism, for instance, the debate crystallizes around the terms *pravṛtti* (or action) and *nivṛtti* (or renunciation) as modes of gaining serenity.

Other views on how life should be lived to maximize serenity were also developed within Taoism. One of these is represented by the "pure conversation" school, which came to believe in refined conversation as the ultimate way to serenity. We have all experienced the sense of serenity which abides when there is no dissension at the dining table!

The school enshrines an important insight — that much of our contact with the world is verbal, so that the cultivation of this aspect of life could be conducive to serenity in a major way.

Another approach to serenity, coming out of the Tao Te Ching, was one which may have been called resignation but for the remarkable fact that it is a sense of resignation which *transcends* both fate and effort. Consider, for instance, the following dialogue between effort and fate — in the Lieh Tzu:

> Effort said to Fate: How can your achievement be compared to mine?
>
> Fate said: What have you done for things that you wish to compare yourself with me?
>
> Effort said: Longevity, brevity of life, obscurity, prominence, honour, humble station, poverty, and success are all within my power.
>
> Fate said: P'eng-tzu's wisdom was not superior to that of Yao and Shun, but he enjoyed a longevity of 800 years. The talent of Yen Hui [Confucius' favourite pupil] was not inferior to those of multitude, yet he lived for only thirty-two years. . . . If such things are within your power, why is it that you allot long life to P'eng-tzu but short life to Yen Hui; that you award

The idea of attaining the mean is developed in a way here which is interesting and different from the Confucian understanding of it. For Confucius too "to go too far is as bad as to fall short." But now this underhitting or overshooting the mark is more clearly related to capacity.

The result of following such a natural course of action is to raise one to a plane of existence where serenity reigns supreme and one becomes proof against the effects of the vicissitudes of fortune and life.

> Joy and sorrow are the results of gains and losses. A gentleman who profoundly penetrates all things and is in harmony with their transformations will be contented with whatever time may bring. He follows the course of nature in whatever situation he may be. He will be intuitively united with creation. He will be himself wherever he may be. Where does gain or loss, life or death, come in? Therefore, if one lets what he has received from nature take its own course, there will be no place for joy or sorrow.[11]

> If one is contented wherever he goes, he will be at ease wherever he may be. Even life and death cannot affect him, much less flood or fire. The perfect man is not besieged by calamities, not because he escapes from them but because he advances the principles of things and goes forward and naturally comes into union with good fortune.[12]

The search for serenity continues in Chuang-Tzu. But the nature of the search is affected by the somewhat different overall orientation of the new text. In the Tao Te Ching, while the immanent aspect of the Tao is recognized, it is the transcendent

---

11. Ibid., p. 245.
12. Ibid., p. 246.

aspect which is emphasized. One has only to recall the opening lines of the text to be confirmed in this:

> The Tao that can be told of is not the eternal Tao;
> The name that can be named is not the eternal name.
> The Nameless is the origin of Heaven and earth;
> The Named is the mother of all things.
>
> Therefore let there always be non-being, so we may see their subtlety,
> And let there always be being, so we may see their outcome.
> The two are the same,
> But after they are produced, they have different names.
> They both may be called deep and profound.
> Deeper and more profound,
> The door of all subtleties!

Comment

This is the most important of all chapters, for in one stroke the basic characteristics of Tao as the eternal, the nameless, the source, and the substance of all things are explicitly or implicitly affirmed. It is no wonder the opening sentences are among the most often quoted or even chanted sayings in Chinese.

The key Taoist concepts of the named and the nameless are also introduced here. The concept of name is common to all ancient Chinese philosophical schools, but Taoism is unique in this respect. Most schools insist on the correspondence of names and actualities and accept names as necessary and good; Taoism, on the contrary, rejects names in favour of the nameless. This, among other things, shows its radical and unique character. To Lao Tzu, Tao is nameless and is the simplicity without names; when names

> arise, that is, when the simple oneness of Tao is split up into individual things with names, it is time to stop.[13]

The tone in which Chuang-Tzu treats of Tao is rather different.

> Whereby is the Tao visited that there should be a distinction of true and false? Whereby is speech vitiated that there should be a distinction of right and wrong? How could the Tao depart and be not there? And how could there be speech and yet it be not appropriate? The Tao is vitiated by petty virtues. Speech is vitiated by flowery eloquence. So it is that we have the contentions between the Confucianists and the Mo-ists, each affirming what the other denies and denying what the other affirms. But if we are to decide on their several affirmations and denials, there is nothing better than to employ the light of reason.
>
> Everything is its own self; everything is something else's other. Things do not know that they are other things' other; they only know that they are themselves. Thus it is said, the other arises out of the self, just as the self arises out of the other. This is the theory that self and other give rise to each other. Besides, where there is life, there is death; and where there is death, there is life. Where there is impossibility, there is possibility; and where there is possibility, there is impossibility. It is because there is right, that there is wrong; it is because there is wrong, that there is right. This being the situation, the sages do not approach things at this level, but reflect the light of nature. Thereupon the self is also the other; the other is also the self. According to the other there is one kind of right and wrong. According to the self there is another kind of right and wrong. But really are there such distinctions as the self and the other, or are there no such distinctions? When the self and the other [or the this and

---

13. Wing Tsit Chan, tr., *The Way of Lao Tzu,* New York: Bobbs-Merrill Company Inc., 1963, p. 97.

> the that] lose their contrariety, there we have the very essence of the Tao. Only the essence of the Tao may occupy the centre of the circle, and respond therefrom to the endless opinions from all directions. Affirmation [of the self] is one of the endless opinions; denial [of the other] is another. Therefore it is said that there is nothing better than to employ the right of reason.[14]

In other words while, for Lao-Tzu, the Tao denotes transcendence and eternity, for Chuang-Tzu it denotes immanence and mutability. Chuang-Tzu "conceives of the universe as a great current in which one state succeeds another in endless procession." How is one to achieve serenity in the midst of such flux?

> In this process of rapid change, everything must follow its own nature. It is the nature of the eagle to fly high in the clouds, the nature of the dove to hop from tree to tree. A cypress will last for a thousand years, a mushroom for only a day. Each should live according to its nature. Similarly a man should be contented with his fate and "should not attempt to replace the way of heaven with the way of man." This is the true meaning of wu-wei. Though there is a much stronger element of fatalism in Chuang-tzu than in Lao-tzu, following Nature to him does not mean blind submission but rather a realistic recognition of one's own limits.
>
> In the universe, then, there are these individual and continuous transformations, each in its own natural way. Such a universal process of rising and falling, of life and death, inevitably result in a world of differences and inequality, but all these are superficial, relative, often products of subjective points of view. Life and death cause each other, and neither right nor wrong is absolute. This

14. Wm. Theodore de Bary, et al., op. cit., pp. 68-69.

and that, and possibility and impossibility, Chuang-tzu says, mutually produce each other. In reality, "all things are one," for Tao embraces all of them and combines into a unity. A man of small knowledge will cut things up, discriminate and make distinctions; a man of great knowledge will be comprehensive, impartial, and see Tao in all its unity. The ideal man will be a "companion with Nature" and a "friend of both life and death." He makes oneness his eternal abode. He abandons selfishness of all descriptions, be it fame, wealth, bias, or subjectivity. He knows his nature, nourishes it, and adapts it to the universal process of transformation. In this way he can "roam the universe" and be "emancipated." Having attained enlightenment through "the light of Nature," he moves in the realm of "great knowledge" and "profound virtue." He is then spiritually free. As the Chuang-tzu itself says of him.

> Alone he associates with heaven and earth and spirit, without abandoning or despising things of the world. He does not quarrel over right or wrong and mingles with conventional society. . . . Above, he roams with the Creator, and below he makes friends with those who transcend life and death and beginning and end. In regard to the essential, he is broad and comprehensive, profound and unrestrained. In regard to the fundamental, he may be said to have harmonized all things and penetrated the highest level. However, in his response to change and its understanding of things, his principle is inexhaustible, traceless, dark and obscure, and unfathomable.[15]

In this respect the image of the horse[16] may be contrasted

15. *Encyclopedia Britannica,* vol. 21, Chicago: William Benton, 1967, pp. 678-79.

16. See Herrlee G. Creel, *What is Taoism and Other Studies in Chinese Cultural History,* Chicago: University of Chicago Press, 1970, chapter 8 for the role of the horse in Chinese history.

with that of the water. According to Chuang-Tzu life goes on "galloping like a horse." Kuo Hsiang develops the views of Chuang-Tzu with the help of the equestrian metaphor:

> The expert driver utilizes the natural capacity of horses to its limit. To use the capacity to its limit lies in letting it take its own course. If forced to run at a rapid pace, with the expectation that they can exceed their capacity, horses will be unable to bear it and many will die. On the other hand, if both worn-out and thoroughbred horses are allowed to use their proper strength and to adapt their pace to their given lot, even if they travel to the borders of the country, their nature will be fully preserved. But there are those who, upon hearing the doctrine of allowing the nature of horses to take its own course, will say: "Then set the horses free and do not ride on them"; and there are those who, upon hearing the doctrine of taking no action, will immediately say: "It is better to lie down than to walk." Why are they so much off the track and unable to return? In this they have missed Chuang Tzu's ideas to a very high degree. — Sec.9, 4:Iib[17]

It seems appropriate to conclude this chapter with a brief passage cited earlier.

> If one is contented wherever he goes, he will be at ease wherever he may be. Even life and death cannot affect him, much less flood or fire. The perfect man is not besieged by calamities, not because he escapes from them but because he advances the principles of things and goes forward and naturally comes into union with good fortune.
>
> — Sec.I, I:I4a[18]

---

17. Wm. Theodore de Bary, et al., eds., op.cit., pp. 245-46.
18. Ibid.

5

The Quest for Serenity in Judaism

THE search for serenity in Judaism proceeds at two levels, the communal and the individual. It is widely held in scholarly circles that the early form of Judaism involved the salvation of Jews as a people, so that the circumstances in which serenity was sought were such as involved the Jews as a people. During the early period, "We have to distinguish between Jewish predictions of the fate of the nation or what the world might be at the end of the age on the one hand, and the destiny of the individual at the end of his existence on the other. Biblical literature abounds with examples of the first, but we come up practically empty-handed when looking for the second."[1] The search for serenity at the individual level does also figure in Jewish literature but at a later stage. We shall address the communal level first on account of its historical priority.

A sense of serenity of the Jewish community at the communal level may be said to correspond to the sense of serenity at the level of the individual. This was seriously threatened in 586 BCE when the Babylonia invaded Judea, razed Solomon's temple to the ground and exiled the leaders of Judean society to Babylon. The Jews up to this point had seen

1. Alan F. Segal, "The Jewish Tradition," in Willard G. Oxtoby, ed., *World Religions: Western Traditions*, 2nd edn., Toronto: Oxford University Press, 2002, pp. 65-66.

themselves in a special covenantal relationship with God — which involved their obeying the laws laid down by Him on their part, and God protecting them on His part.

The destruction of the kingdom and exile from Jerusalem meant that this dispensation did not hold any more. As Alan Segal puts it:

> The destruction of the temple brought on a crisis of confidence. It stemmed not from Yahweh's being viewed as a regional God only, for he was also lord of all creation, but from his having been worshipped in a single, principal sanctuary for so long. With that building destroyed, had Yahweh finally abandoned his people? The author of *Lamentations* 5:20-2 puts it:
>
> Why dost thou forget us forever, why
> dost thou so long forsake us?
> Restore us to thyself, O Lord, that we may
> be restored! Renew our days as of old!
> Or hast thou utterly rejected us? Art thou
> exceedingly angry with us?
>
> The nation needed a sign that God had not permanently rejected it. As if in response, the prophet Ezekiel describes a heavenly chariot driven by the glory of God. In Ezekiel's bizarre vision, Yahweh's heavenly chariot and the radiance of divine presence appear in a storm cloud, just as in the Canaanite-like imagery of *Psalm* 29. Abandoning the temple just before its destruction, God's presence approaches Babylonia. The concrete, mythological answer to *Psalm* 137's cry above about singing Yahweh's song in a foreign land is that one can do so because he came into exile with the people.[2]

---

2. Ibid., p. 54.

This was followed by an objective piece of evidence that Yahweh had not abandoned the Jews, when Cyrus allowed the Jews to return to Palestine. It is easy to see now how the Jewish presence in Babylon and then subsequent return could be and "was seen by the Israelites living there as part of God's plan" (see *Ezra* 1:1; *Isaiah* 41:2; 44:28, 45:1).[3]

The Jewish communal search for serenity resulted in, and then resulted from the transformation of Yahweh from a God of a given people to the God of the whole world.

> Now Yahweh must direct all world history, not just the destiny of Judah. Cyrus was no exclusive worshipper of Yahweh. But the announcement of return was in keeping with his policy of patronizing the priesthoods and cults of the old order. The writer of *Isaiah* 45 is so impressed that he calls him the "messiah" (the anointed one), designated by Yahweh as his instrument to fulfil Israel's destiny.[4]

In the history of Judaism the security of the community would be tested again and again. And Jews would seek serenity in the face of these crises in similar ways: in seeing God's presence with them in their crises, suffering with them if you will; and as, the God of history, coming to their rescue from time to time, in keeping with his mercy, or allowing them to perish in keeping with his justice. Yet another way they would seek serenity would be in the hope that some day, even soon, a divine, or divinely inspired figure will appear to save them from their perils, thereby enabling them to experience the security, even serenity of a Messianic age. It must be added, however, that the exile experience of the Jews has been so prolonged, and the experience so profound, that some have

3. Ibid.
4. Ibid., p. 55.

sought serenity in that very state. As R.J. Zwi Werblowsky notes:

> There seems to be a religious dimension to the sociological fact that Jewry has polarized in two centres — Israel and America. The two centres represent the two classical forms of Jewish life — the Judaism of the Diaspora and the Judaism of the nation in its own homeland. Both are historical configurations which Israel has known as forms of the covenant.[5]

The recognition of the exile as a form of the covenant would seem to be a primary manifestation of the Jewish search for serenity at the communal level. The idea that they were a "chosen people" would conduce to serenity even in such times of trials, including the Holocaust.

The Book of Job is a paradigmatic example of the Jewish search for serenity at the individual level. The account is well known but may be briefly recounted. Job was a pious Jew who was a model of faith and rectitude but Satan persuaded God to let him be tested by Satan, with the stipulation that Job may be tested as thoroughly as Satan wishes but his life be spared. Job loses his possessions and is then afflicted with sores but does not curse God even though the friends who visit him point out he has every reason to. He is, however, plagued by the question: why me? And this quest for an answer finally leads to a colloquy with God.[6]

---

5. R.J. Zwi Werblowsky, "Judaism, or The Religion of Israel," in R.C. Zaehner, ed., *The Concise Encyclopedia of Living Faiths*, Boston: Beacon Press, 1967, p. 49, emphasis added.
6. Herbert G. May and Bruce M. Metzer, eds., *The New Oxford Annotated Bible with The Apocrypha*, New York: Oxford University Press, 1977, pp. 613-55.

Job's search for serenity is then everyone's search for serenity, when the serene pace of our life is disturbed by unaccountable painful happenings.

Scholars have read several possible answers in this famous text. There is the suggestion that the sheer finitude of human beings puts God's workings beyond their understanding and serenity is to be found in the acceptance of God's inscrutable glory. It had also been suggested that "God has not justified *Job*, but he has come to him personally; the upholder of the universe cares for a lonely man so deeply that he offers him the fullness of his communion. *Job* is not vindicated but he has obtained far more than a recognition of his innocence: he has been accepted by the ever-present master-worker, and the intimacy with the Creator makes vindication superfluous."[7]

This theologically Zen path is not the only one leading to serenity. The fact that good fortune is restored to *Job* may convince some that God is just, which has been a source of serenity, inasmuch as it generates the confidence that delay should not lead to disillusionment so far as justice is concerned.

---

7. Ibid., pp. 654-55. "As for the author of Ecclesiastes, all that seemed to him good he summed up in such words as these: "I know there is nothing good for man but to be glad and enjoy himself while he lives." Everything else involved futility, a vain striving to hold the wind. Perhaps the writer had read the older book, *Job*, and had been unable to solve its fundamental problem: Why does not God make it the rule that the righteous prosper and the wicked suffer? But no, the righteous suffer and the wicked prosper. *Ecclesiastes* only vaguely catches *Job*'s suggestion that the wise and pure in heart may transcend their suffering by rejoicing in the wisdom and majesty of God revealed in the awesome design of the world." John B. Noss, *Man's Religions*, 6th edn., New York: The Macmillan Company, Inc., 1980, p. 389.

The source of serenity however which ultimately evolved at the level of the individual was that of resurrection, the first "indisputable reference" to which is found in the Book of Daniel 12:2.

> And many of those who sleep in the dust of the earth shall awake, some to everlasting life, and some to shame and everlasting contempt. And those who are wise shall shine like the brightness of the firmament; and those who turn many to righteousness, like the stars forever and ever.
>
> Those who suffered and died in remaining true to God's Torah will be vindicated. The reference to the saved as "sleepers in the dust" may be a reinterpretation of *Isaiah* 26:19. The Jewish expectation among the first-century Jewish followers of Jesus that he might survive death on the cross is understandable if they regarded him as a martyr.
>
> The doctrine of resurrection is this-worldly in orientation, imagining the next life to be comparable to the present one. But injustice is removed, with the next realm attending to unfinished business from the present one. Those who persecuted the righteous of Yahweh must be resurrected too, so that they can be punished.[8]

---

8. Alan Segal, op. cit., p. 68. The doctrine evolved over a period of time (ibid., pp. 67-68): "Nothing in Hebrew thought anticipates the post-biblical ideas of paradise or resurrection as a reward for a righteous life. When the possibility is raised as a direct issue, the answer seems to be no. Consider *Ecclesiastes* 3:19: "For the fate of the sons of men and the fate of beasts is the same; as one dies, so does the other. They all have the same breath, and man has no advantage over the beasts; for all is vanity."

   Another passage, though often read as a prediction of *Job*'s resurrection, appears only to affirm that *Job* wants to be vindicated while still alive. *Job* seeks an advocate in a heavenly court, as the logical outcome of his challenge to the justice of God.

→

In these ways Judaism offered the hope of serenity to its followers both as a community and as individuals.

→ For I know that my Redeemer (or Vindicator) lives; and at last he will stand upon the earth;
and after my skin has been thus destroyed, then from my flesh I shall see God,
whom I shall see on my side, and my eyes shall behold, and not another. — *Job* 19:25-6

Job, like *Ecclesiastes*, seems almost to argue explicitly against any simple pietistic belief in immortality, in direct contradiction to the way the book is usually understood today.

In the later prophetic books especially, the Canaanite mythological battle between Death and Ba'al is reused as an allegory of the power of Yahweh. *Isaiah* 25:8 says, "God will swallow up death forever." *Isaiah* 26 and *Ezekiel* 37 speak of the restoration of the people as a resurrection of buried bones, but nothing in these verses implies the expectation of an individual resurrection. The metaphor of resurrection is explicitly interpreted as a description of a corporate renewal.

Judaism evidently developed the doctrine of resurrection in response to the problem of martyrdom. Martyrdom became an option only when one was asked to risk death specifically for one's religion, rather than for other interests, a development we locate in the Maccabean revolt."

only did he dedicate his life to the propagation of Christianity, but his own life was also transformed. The acceptance of Jesus Christ as the saviour had the effect of relieving him of anxiety in all its forms. This is dramatically illustrated by the incident when he remained totally serene in the presence of the serpent.

The serenity with which the early Christians faced the persecution at the hands of the Romans can also be seen as basically rooted in the belief that sin and death had been overcome through faith in Jesus Christ. The fear of both physical and spiritual death afflicts us in many subtle forms. J.G. Jung is said to have maintained that all psychological ailments after the age of forty had their root in this fear. If the fear of death is such a fundamental fear then Christianity shows considerable perception in emphasizing that, for the Christian, death has been overcome through the resurrection of Jesus Christ.

Christian motives contribute to serenity in other ways as well. Apart from relieving the ontological anxiety about life, one is relieved of the lesser anxieties of life by placing them in a high ethical perspective. The injunction of returning evil with good, for instance, certainly contributes to the serenity of one who practises it, as does the other Christian virtue of forgiveness. The Lord's Prayer blends many serene aspects of Christianity. The whole section which follows it in the Sermon on the Mount is also relevant here:

> Our father in heaven,
> Thy name be hallowed:
> Thy kingdom come,
> Thy will be done,
> On earth as in heaven.
> Give us today our daily bread.
> Forgive us the wrong we have done,
> As we have forgiven those who have wronged us.

And do not bring us to the test,
But save us from the evil one.

For if you forgive others the wrongs they have done, your heavenly Father will also forgive you; but if you do not forgive others, then the wrongs you have done will not be forgiven by your Father.

So too when you fast, do not look gloomy like hypocrites; they make their faces unsightly so that other people may see that they are fasting. I tell you this: they have their reward already. But when you fast, anoint your head and wash your face, so that men may not see that you are fasting, but only your Father who is in the secret place; and your Father who sees what is secret will give you your reward.

Do not store up for yourselves treasure on earth, where it grows rusty and moth-eaten, and thieves break in to steal it. Store up treasure in heaven, where there is no moth and no rust to spoil it, no thieves to break in and steal. For where your wealth is, there will your heart be also.

The lamp of the body is the eye. If your eyes are sound, you will have light for your whole body; if the eyes are bad, your whole body will be in darkness. If then the only light you have is darkness, the darkness is doubly dark.

No servant can be slave to two masters; for either he will hate the first and love the second, or he will be devoted to the first and think nothing of the second. You cannot serve God and Money.

Therefore I bid you put away anxious thoughts about food and drink to keep you alive, and clothes to cover your body. Surely life is more than food, the body more than clothes. Look at the birds of the air; they do not sow and reap and store in barns, yet your heavenly Father feeds them. You are worth more than the birds! Is there a man of you who by anxious thought can add a foot to his height? And why be

> anxious about clothes? Consider how the lilies grow in the fields; they do not work, they do not spin; and yet, I tell you, even Solomon in all his splendour was not attired like one of these. But if that is how God clothes the grass in the fields, which is there today, and tomorrow is thrown on the stove, will he not all the more clothe you? How little faith you have! No, do not ask anxiously, "What have we to eat? What have we to drink? What shall we wear?" All these things are for the heathen to run after, not for you, because your heavenly Father knows that you need them all. Set your mind on God's kingdom and his justice before everything else, and all the rest will come to you as well. So do not be anxious about tomorrow; tomorrow will look after itself. Each day has troubles enough of its own.[1]

In the search for serenity in Christianity the idea of the fatherhood of God would seem to play as important a part as that of the divine sonship and sacrifice of Jesus Christ. As a matter of fact, it was to God as father (*abbā*) that Jesus himself turned in his less serene moments.[2] Freudian psychology had brought this idea of the fatherhood of God into disrepute. It almost suggests, if it does not say so, that perhaps Jesus was an illegitimate son who did not know his father and therefore suffered from a father-fixation. Apart from being unduly speculative, it seems that such a view overlooks the psychologically healing quality of a parent-child relationship. As children, some of our most serene moments are spent with our parents.

---

1. T. Patrick Burke, *The Major Religions: An Introduction with Texts*, Oxford: Blackwell Publishers Inc., 1996, pp. 317-18.
2. J.G. Davies, "Christianity: The Early Church," in R.C. Zaehner, ed., *The Concise Encyclopedia of Living Faiths*, Boston: Beacon Press, 1967, pp. 53-54.

The search for serenity in Christianity has an interesting angle to it. Sometimes serenity is sought not through the providence of God but through the allied belief that everything is divinely predestined. The idea that everything is preordained can be a source of serenity, but it can also deprive one of it if one then proceeds to fret over the fact. What then becomes of my free will or at least of the sense that I possess free will even if in some sense I may not possess it.

Some thinkers of Christianity developed an interesting position on this point, that a person's freedom of will could be reconciled with belief in God's foreknowledge. The thoughts of the Christian Roman philosopher, Ancius Boethius (*c.* 480-524), are particularly relevant in this regard. He begins by acknowledging the apparent contradiction between the two — God's universal foreknowledge and freedom of will — as follows:

> Well, the two seem clean contrary and opposite, God's universal foreknowledge and freedom of the will. If God foresees all things and cannot be mistaken in any way, what Providence has foreseen as a future event must happen. So that if from eternity Providence foreknows not only men's actions but also their thoughts and desires, there will be no freedom of will. No action or desire will be able to exist other than that which God's infallible Providence has foreseen. For if they can be changed and made different from how they were foreseen, there will be no sure foreknowledge of the future, only an uncertain opinion; and this I do not think can be believed of God.[3]

Boethius resolves this contradiction in two steps. His first step is to emphasize that while for us all events occur in past,

3. V.E. Watts, tr., *Boethius: The Consolation of Philosophy*, Hardmonsworth: Penguin Books Ltd., 1969, p. 150. I am indebted to Professor Torrance Kirby to this and subsequent references.

present, or future because we are subject to time, God dwells in eternity which is beyond time and in which only the present exists. His second step consists of distinguishing between two kinds of acts in our present — those which are characterized by necessity, like the movement of the sun across the sky, and those which are freely willed, like someone's decision in the present, to walk one way rather than the other. Note that although it is a freely willed decision by anyone to walk one way rather than the other in the present, his action, in whichever direction it be, is known to us in the present, although it is freely willed. Since for God only the present exists, he thus has correct knowledge of both kinds of actions. As Boethius puts it:

> And if human and divine present may be compared, as you see certain things in this your present time, so God sees all things in His eternal present. So that this divine foreknowledge does not change the nature and property of things; it simply sees things present to it exactly as they will happen at some time as future events. It makes no confused judgements of things, but with one glance of its mind distinguishes all that is to come to pass whether it is necessitated or not. Similarly you, when you see at the same time a man walking on the earth and the sun rising in the sky, although the two sights coincide yet you distinguish between them and judge the one to be willed and the other necessitated. In the same way the divine gaze looks down on all things without disturbing their nature; to Him they are present things. And so it comes about that when God knows that something is going to occur and knows that no necessity is to be imposed upon it, it is not opinion, but rather knowledge founded upon truth.[4]

---

4. Ibid., pp. 165-66.

7

The Quest for Serenity in Islam

THE quest for serenity in Islam begins with the recitation of the Koran itself, even before we get to the meaning of what is being recited. This statement runs the risk of sounding far-fetched, so allow me to substantiate it with the experience of Driss Charaibi, the author of an autobiographical novel entitled, *Heirs To The Past*. The occasion is the return of the émigré son for the funeral of his father.

> Then a man stood up . . . and began to chant. What he chanted was of no importance. It was not the words, nor the meaning, nor even the symbolism, which moved our hearts, the men, women and children who were there. We forgot why we were there the moment he began to chant. It was the incantation, and the end of our woes and miserable little problems, the aching and yet serene longing for that other life which is ours and to which we are all destined to return, the victors and the defeated, the fully developed and those who are still at the larva state, the faithful and the atheists, through God's great compassion. There was all of that in the voice of the man who stood chanting in the sun, and we were in his voice, I was in his voice despite the vast legacy of incredibility that I had received from the West. When he reached the end of a verse, he paused, and so it came about — an outburst of fervor. And while he chanted it was like a man in the wilderness chanting his faith. And the voice rose and swelled, changed in tone, became tragic, soared and then

> floated down on our heads like a seagull gliding gently and softly, little more than a whisper. And so — never again will I go in search of intellectuals, of written truths, synthetic truths, of collections of hybrid ideas which are nothing but ideas. Never again will I travel the world in search of a shadow of justice, fairness, progress, or schemes calculated to change mankind. I was weary and I was returning to my clan. The man who was not even aware of his voice or of his faith was alive and held the secret of life — a man who could not even have been a dustman in this world of founts of knowledge and civilization. Peace and everlasting truth were in him and in his voice, while all was crumbling around him on the continents.[1]

The search for serenity in Islam is basically centred on the relation of man's will to God's will. As noted earlier, however, this is not just true of only Islam but also of Judaism and Christianity. There are, however, differences in nuance between the three religious traditions on this point. Moreover, the doctrine of God's will also undergoes its own particular elaboration in Islam and it will be useful to examine the extent to which this new elaboration contributes to the achievement of serenity.

It was pointed out earlier that in Judaism the search for serenity results in the acceptance both of the laws and of the majestic mystery of God. Typically God answers Job not by answering his question like a professor but by displaying his marvellous powers as a pre-designator. Earlier, Abraham achieves serenity by unquestioning obedience of God by showing his willingness to sacrifice his son. Abraham's unquestioning obedience should not be taken literally, for there is an element of absurdity in God's demand from a purely

---

1. Cited in T. Patrick Burke, *The Major Religions: An Introduction with Texts*, Oxford: Blackwell Publishers Ltd., 1996, p. 241.

rational point of view. First of all he answers Abraham's prayers by granting him a son when his wife is past the childbearing age, and then calls him to sacrifice that son to him, thus in effect depriving him of what had been granted to him. Abraham achieves serenity in Judaism by accepting God's will. In Islam Abraham is described as a Muslim, as the word literally means one who submits to the will of God. But while the fact of Abraham's willingness to sacrifice his son is emphasized in the Koran, the son in this case is not Isaac but Ishmael. This to a certain extent weakens the point as Isaac's rather than Ishmael's sacrifice would seem to involve greater devotion on the part of Abraham. From the Islamic point of view, however, the difference may not be material, as the Muslims are believed to have descended from Ishmael. It is clear, therefore, that the central point of Abraham's story from the point of view of Islam is his submission to the will of God. The same point emerges from the treatment of the story of Jesus in the Koran. The passage dealing with the death of Jesus is the subject of much controversy and the literalness of Jesus' crucifixion seems to be denied — but again in the context of God's will. God is said to have willed an apparition in the place of Jesus himself, whom he raised to himself.

It is clear from the Islamic treatment of Judaic and Christian narratives that the will of God is the overriding motive in Islam. How, then, is the search for serenity to be related to this?

Serenity is to be achieved by complete submission to the will of God. At one level, this will of God is made known through the Islamic law or Shari'ah so that serenity can be achieved, and indeed it appears to have been achieved by Muslims by submission to it. At a philosophical rather than a legal level, however, the point can pose some problems. It has been maintained philosophically that everything in this world happens only through the will of God. If this be so, then what scope is there for human will to resist it? And moreover, can human will be exercised at all if all that exists is God's will?

The problem of lack of serenity arises in Islam because man pits his will against God's. Ontologically he is not capable of doing this, but morally he is. And all that man achieves by thus not morally conforming to the will of God — by not obeying the Shari'ah for instance — is to lose serenity not only here but more so in the hereafter.

The fact that ontologically only God's will prevails but morally there is room for human dissidence raises at least three interesting issues. (1) How can man be morally responsible for deeds which are only possible through God's omnipotence? (2) Is man really even morally responsible? (3) Should human will be exercised at all?

According to the orthodox Islamic doctrine man "appropriates" the deeds which can only be performed through God's power, by regarding himself as their performer. This answers the first question. As for the second, man is not "really" responsible but becomes so by the aforesaid appropriation. Thus the real issue, at the highest philosophical level, is not whether man actually possesses free will but his impression that he does. At the practical level, however, man does and should exercise his will. When the prophet was asked by a Bedouin whether he should tie his camel or trust in God, the prophet is believed to have replied that he should tie his camel *and* trust in God.

It is clear that if everything rests on God's will, serenity is achieved by a wholehearted recognition of this fact. The technical word for such self-surrender in Sufism is Tawakkul, although the word Muslim carries the same connotation. In practical conduct this manifests itself in a degree of dependence of God some might find disconcerting:

> A dervish fell into the Tigris. Seeing that he could not swim, a man on the bank cried out, "Shall I tell some one to bring you ashore?" "No," said the dervish. "Then do you wish to be drowned?" "No." "What, then, do you wish?" The dervish replied, "God's will be done! What have I to do with wishing?"[2]

Reynold Nicholson explains:

> "Trust in God," in its extreme form, involves the renunciation of every personal initiative and volition; total passivity like that of a corpse in the hands of the washer who prepares it fit for burial; perfect indifference towards anything that is even remotely connected with one's self. A special class of the ancient Sufis took their name from this "trust," which they applied, so far as they were able, to matters of everyday life. For instance, they would not seek food, work for hire, practise any trade, or allow medicine to be given them when they were ill. Quietly they committed themselves to God's care, never doubting that He, to whom belong the treasure of earth and heaven, would provide for their wants, and that their allotted portion would come to them as surely as it comes to the birds, which neither sow nor reap, and to the fish in the sea, and to the child in the womb.[3]

A loftier example of this attitude is found in the following account of Rabi'a:

> Some one said to Rabi'a: "I have committed many sins; if I turn in penitence towards God, will he turn in mercy towards

---

2. Reynold A. Nicholson, *The Mystics of Islam*, Harmondsworth: Penguin, 1975, p. 41.

3. Ibid., pp. 41-42.

> me?" "Nay," she replied, "but if He shall turn towards thee, thou wilt turn towards Him."[4]

The justification for considering it lofty, if asked for, is as follows:

> The question whether sins ought to be remembered after repentance or forgotten illustrates a fundamental point in Sufi ethics: I mean the difference between what is taught to novices and disciples and what is held as an esoteric doctrine by adepts. Any Mohammedan director of souls would tell his pupils that to think humbly and remorsefully of one's sins is a sovereign remedy against spiritual pride, but he himself might very well believe that real repentance consists in forgetting everything except God.
>
> "The penitent," says Hujwiri, "is a lover of God, and the lover of God is in contemplation of god: in contemplation it is wrong to remember sin, for recollection of sin is a veil between God and the contemplative."
>
> Sin appertains to self-existence, which itself is the greatest of all sins. To forget sin is to forget self.
>
> This is only one application of a principle which, as I have said, runs through the whole ethical system of Sufism and will be more fully explained in a subsequent chapter. Its dangers are evident, but we must in fairness allow that the same theory of conduct may not be equally suitable to those who have made themselves perfect in moral discipline and to those who are still striving after perfection.
>
> Over the gate of repentance it is written:
>
> "All self abandon ye who enter here."[5]

---

4. Ibid., p. 31.
5. Ibid., pp. 31-32.

Sometimes this feeling of utter dependence on God found an expression in the simplicity of the mystic's life.

> Dawud al-Ta'l owned nothing except a mat of rushes, a brick which he used as a pillow, and a leathern vessel which served him for drinking and washing. A certain man dreamed that he saw Malik ibn Dinar and Mohammed ibn Wasi being led into Paradise, and that Malik was admitted before his companion. He cried out in astonishment, for he thought Mohammed ibn Wasi' had a superior claim to the honour. "Yes," came the answer, "but Mohammed ibn Wasi' possessed two shirts, and Malik only one. That is the reason why Malik is preferred."
>
> The Sufi ideal of poverty goes far beyond this. True poverty is not merely lack of wealth, but lack of desire for wealth: the empty heart as well as the empty hand. The "poor man" (*faqīr*) and the "mendicant" (*dervish*) are names by which the Mohammedan mystic is proud to be known, because they imply that he is stripped of every thought or wish that would divert his mind from God.[6]

Thus serenity is achieved in Islam through becoming Allah-centred instead of being self-centred. The "self" rebels against submitting to the will of God, but once it does, complete serenity is achieved. Such submission to the will of God should not be confused with fatalism. The doctrine that everything happens according of the will of god is also moral. God does control the results of our deeds as well. Thus it is the twofold recognition of God's will as ontologically grounding the universe and as morally controlling the results of our actions, which leads to the serene performance of our duties in life.

---

6. Ibid., pp. 36-37.

8

Conclusion

It was the aim of this book to adumbrate the search for serenity in the world religions which conventionally include Hinduism, Buddhism, Confucianism, Taoism, Judaism, Christianity and Islam. And we found that while each religion has its own way of addressing the issue, certain broad similarities can be discerned underlying them.

The most fundamental similarity which may be inferred is in their analysis of the problem, namely, that life presents us with two sets of events, those over which we have control and those over which we don't, although the distinction is a dynamic and subtle one. Thus whether I decide to turn right or left is within my power but whether a car might come and hit me while I am doing so may not be something I have the power to prevent from happening. Life is characterized by events of both these types and this causes anxiety. The various ways in which such anxiety may be replaced by serenity is then discussed by the various religions.

Is then achieving serenity the goal of these religions? The question is difficult to answer but a two-tier approach could be proposed. Most religious traditions insist on the need for a calm mind. The search for such calmness represents the search for serenity at one level. Then there is also the hint, or even promise, that when one approaches life, or searches for reality with such a calm mind, then dimensions of reality are disclosed which impart to our life a sense of serenity at a deeper level, beyond the level of a mind at ease in itself, at a level at which it is at peace with the reality itself.

Bibliography

Bṛhadāraṇyaka Upaniṣad.

Burke, Patrick T., 1996, *The Major Religions: An Introduction with Texts*, Oxford: Blackwell Publishers.

Chan, Wing Tsit, tr., 1963, *The Way of Lao Tzu*, New York: Bobbs-Merrill Company Inc.

Conze, Edward, 1959, "Buddhism," in R.C. Zaehner, ed., *The Concise Encyclopaedia of Living Faiths*, Boston: Beacon Press.

Creel, Herrlee G., 1970, *What is Taoism and Other Studies in Chinese Cultural History*, Chicago: University of Chicago Press.

Davies, J.G., 1967, "Christianity: The Early Church," in R.C. Zaehner, ed., op. cit.

De Bary, Wm. Theodore, ed., 1960, *Sources of Chinese Tradition*, New York and London: Columbia University Press.

Durant, Will, 1954, *Our Oriental Heritage*, New York: Simon and Schuster.

Edgerton, Franklin, tr., 1946, *The Bhagavad-Gītā*, Cambridge: Massachusetts: Harvard University Press.

Encyclopaedia Britannica, 1967, Chicago: William Benton.

Fromm, Erich, 1950, *Psychoanalysis and Religion*, New Haven: Yale University Press.

Graham, A.C., 1967, "Confucianism," in R.C. Zaeher, ed., op. cit.

Hill, W. Douglas O., 1971, *The Holy Lake of the Acts of Rama*, Delhi: Oxford University Press.

Hiriyanna, M., 1949, *The Essentials of Indian Philosophy*, London: George Allen & Unwin Ltd.

Hume, Robert Ernest, tr., 1968, *The Thirteen Principal Upaniṣads*, London: Oxford University Press.

May, Herbert G. and Metzer, Bruce M., eds., 1977, *The New Annotated Bible with the Apocrypha*, New York: Oxford University Press.

Nicholson, Reynold A., 1975, *The Mystics of Islam*, Hardmonsworth: Penguin Books.

Noss, John B., 1980, *Man's Religions*, 6th edn., New York: The Macmillan Company.

Rahula, Walpola, 1974, *What the Buddha Taught*, New York: Grove Press, Inc.

Reps, Paul, compiler, 1961, *Zen Flesh, Zen Bones*, New York: Doubleday and Company Inc.

Sambuddhananda, Swami, 1959, *Vedanta Through Stories*, Bombay: Sri Ramakrishna Ashram.

Segal, Alan F., 2002, "The Jewish Tradition," in Willard G. Oxtoby, ed., *World Religions: Western Traditions*, 2nd edn., Toronto: Oxford University Press.

Smith, Huston, *The Religions of Man*, New York: Harper & Row.

Thompson, Laurence G., 1975, *Chinese Religion: An Introduction*, Belmont, California: Dickenson Publishing Company Inc.

Waley, Arthur, tr., 1938, *The Analects of Confucius*, New York: Random House.

Walker, Benjamin, 1968, *The Hindu World*, New York: Frederick A. Praeger.

Watts, V.E., tr., 1969, *The Consolation of Philosophy*, Hardmonsworth: Penguin Books.

Werblowsky, R.J. Zwi, 1967, "Judaism or the Religion of Israel," in R.C. Zaehner, ed., op. cit.

Index

Note: The word 'Serenity' was omitted, since it is the 'subject' of the book.